# HEART
OF A
# COACH™
# PLAYBOOK

## DAILY DEVOTIONS FOR
## LEADING BY EXAMPLE

**Regal**

For more information and
special offers from Regal Books, email us at
subscribe@regalbooks.com

Published by Regal
From Gospel Light
Ventura, California, U.S.A.
*www.regalbooks.com*
Printed in the U.S.A.

**Library of Congress Cataloging-in-Publication Data**
The heart of a coach playbook :
daily devotions for leading by example.
pages cm
ISBN 978-0-8307-6869-1 (pbk.)
1. Sports—Religious aspects—Christianity.
2. Coaches (Athletics)—Religious life.  I. Regal Books.
GV706.42.H43 2013
796.07'7—dc23
2013028657

Rights for publishing this book outside the U.S.A. or in
non-English languages are administered by Gospel Light
Worldwide, an international not-for-profit ministry. For
additional information, please visit www.glww.org, email
info@glww.org, or write to Gospel Light Worldwide,
1957 Eastman Avenue, Ventura, CA 93003, U.S.A.

To order copies of this book and other Regal products in
bulk quantities, please contact us at 1-800-446-7735.

# Contents

# Good Reminders

I have supported the Fellowship of Christian Athletes almost from its beginning. Through the ensuing years, I have attended and spoken at many FCA meetings—including the Key to Life Award Banquet—and my children and grandchildren have enjoyed going to FCA camps.

One year, I heard a minister named Bob Menielly speak at an FCA event at Estes Park. He is the person who first gave me a poem titled "God's Hall of Fame." I memorized that poem and have referred to it many times through the years.

In 1964, my UCLA team won our first NCAA men's basketball championship. The final game was in Kansas City, Missouri. In those days, it was played on a Saturday, not on a Monday as it is today. We capped an undefeated season by beating Duke 98-83. I was feeling pretty good.

The next day was Easter Sunday, and I wanted to hear Bob Menielly speak at his church, which was near Kansas City. With my assistant coach and our wives, we headed off to the service. As we walked from the car to the sanctuary, a pigeon scouted out our little group, no doubt noticing that we were wearing our Sunday bests, including fashionable hats. The pigeon's aim was perfect. Plop, his little gift of humility landed right on top of my new hat. Here my team had just won the national championship and I was feeling very pleased with life, and along came the pigeon. I think he was a messenger, perhaps from God. From that point on, I always kept in mind my proper place, even after winning championships.

I do not tell this story often, but I think that it is a good reminder for anyone who is a coach. After all, it is our humility that enables us to control our emotions during the good times and the bad. It is good to have other reminders, too. Since 1942, I have carried a small cross in my pocket. No, it is not a good luck charm; rather, it is a reminder. Whenever I place my hand in my pocket and grasp that cross, my proper perspective returns. If we are at peace with Christ, we will not be so wrapped up with ourselves, nor will we be so vulnerable to the ups and downs of a particular practice, game or season. We will build a shelter for eternity rather than an E-Z Up® canopy that we fold up after each game.

Every day, I read the Bible. I also read books, poems and devotions—most anything of value. Each night, when I go to bed, I recite poetry until I fall asleep. What I read and what I recite serve as reminders, like the pigeon and the cross. Words of inspiration remind me that real success does not come from the number of championships a coach wins, the size of his or her contract, or the level of his or her fame. Words of reassurance remind me that success only comes when, at the end of the day, we have peace of mind and peace with God.

Before you is a wonderful book of devotional readings. I encourage you to read one each day. Let them remind, teach and speak to you about character, truth and all that really matters in the heart of a coach. Use them as you seek to be an example to your players and a keeper of the faith. Let them help bring you the peace of mind that comes when you have peace with God.

John Wooden
Head Basketball Coach, 1948-1975
UCLA

Dear Coach,

Since 1954, FCA has been privileged to minister to coaches by encouraging and equipping them to know and serve the Master Coach, Jesus Christ.

Coaching is all about relationships. Whether it's a player, a fellow coach or our family, the only way to get to know a person is to spend time with him or her. These devotions are designed to help you develop a focused time with God. Each is written from a coach's point of view to help you understand God's perspective on issues you face as a coach. Our hope is that this book will deepen your understanding of His Word and your calling as a coach.

As a coach, you have been given a tremendous platform to influence others. May God use this playbook to transform your life as a coach so that you can make an eternal impact for Jesus Christ.

Your Teammate in Christ,

Les Steckel
FCA President/CEO

# Training Time

In sports, time-outs give coaches a chance to strategize for upcoming challenges. Similarly, in life, we need to take time-outs to think about our purpose as members of God's team. FCA is excited to present you with a collection of devotions that will challenge you to coach and live for the glory of God. Each devotion is written from a coach's perspective and will encourage you to be more like Christ both on and off the field or court of competition.

Every morning, set aside a special quiet time to be with God. During this spiritual training time, talk to God and let Him speak to you through the Bible. There are many effective methods that can be used for your daily time with God. One method that we recommend is the PRESS method.

## The PRESS Method

### Pray

Begin your quiet time by thanking God for the new day, and then ask Him to help you learn from what you're about to read. Prepare yourself by:

- clearing your mind and being quiet before the Lord

- asking God to settle your heart

- listening to worship music to prepare your spirit

- asking God to give you a teachable heart

### Read

Begin with the 31 devotionals provided in this book. Also, try reading a chapter of Proverbs every day (there are 31 chapters in the book of Proverbs, which makes it ideal for daily reading), one psalm and/or a chapter out of the Old or New Testament. You may consider beginning with one of the Gospels (Matthew, Mark, Luke or John), or one of the shorter letters, such as Ephesians or James.

### Examine

Ask yourself the following questions with regard to the passage you read:

- *Teaching:* What do I need to *know* about God, myself and others?

- *Rebuking:* What do I need to *stop* doing—sins, habits or selfish patterns?

- *Correcting:* What do I need to *change* in my thoughts, attitudes or actions?

- *Training:* What do I need to *do* in obedience to God's leading?

## Summarize

Do one of the following:

- Discover what the passage reveals about God and His character, what it says or promises about you, and what it says or promises about others (such as your family, friends or players). Write your thoughts down in a personal journal.

- Rewrite one or two key verses in your own words.

- Outline what each verse is saying.

- Give each verse a one-word title that summarizes what it says.

## Share

Talk with God about what you've learned. Also, take time each day to share with another person what you learned during that day's study. Having a daily training time is the key to spiritual development. If you commit to working through these 31 devotionals over the next month, you will establish this as a habit—one that will be vital to your growth in Christ.

If you are committed to establishing this daily training time with God, fill out the box below.

*I will commit to establishing a daily habit of spending time with God.*

Signed _____

Today's Date _____

## Writers

We have invited FCA staff, coaches and team chaplains from all levels to contribute their time, talent and experience in writing these devotions. These writers come from diverse backgrounds and include representatives from a variety of sports, including baseball, soccer, basketball, football, lacrosse, track and field, and others. You can check out our writers' biographies in the Contributors section at the end of the book.

## Format

**Ready**     A verse or passage of Scripture that focuses or directs your heart and mind. Turn to the Scripture reference in your Bible and read it within the overall context of the passage.

**Set**
A teaching point (a story, training point or thought taken from a sports perspective) that draws a lesson from the passage.

**Go**
Questions that will help you examine your heart and challenge you to apply God's truth to your life—on and off the field or court.

**Workout**
Additional Scripture references to help you dig deeper.

**Overtime**
A closing prayer that will help you commit to the Lord what you have learned.

To RECEIVE THE DAILY EMAIL DEVOTIONAL
**"FCA's Impact Play,"** go to www.FCA.org.

# 1

# Correct, Don't Criticize

## Ready

*For the Lord disciplines the one He loves,*
*just as a father, the son he delights in.*
PROVERBS 3:12

## Set

When I first started working towards becoming a head coach, people wondered if I could do it. I wasn't the type to yell at people. I wasn't the type to get in people's faces. They didn't know if I could control the players. How would they respond to my coaching style? How would I handle being in charge of an entire team?

My style has always been one that relies on motivation, encouragement and teaching. I always want to help people get better. That's the idea behind correction. It's not about tearing people down. It's about helping them improve. You have to let them know when they've done something wrong, but the goal is to help them become a better player and a better person.

There are certain things that are going to be done a certain way and they're not negotiable. The punishment is already set and everyone knows it. But then, if a rule is broken and you have to correct, it's best to avoid sharp criticisms, but instead to discipline with love. That approach gives the person the best opportunity to change his or her behavior.

Jesus corrected by telling stories. He showed examples. He pointed things out. He didn't just say, "This is wrong and this is right." He corrected people by getting them to think. When He corrected His disciples, they walked away understanding that it was for their benefit.

As a society, we desperately need to develop young people who are correctable. The youth generation is sometimes difficult to correct because of the way they've gotten correction. They have rebelled against correction because they see it as criticism. When the time for discipline comes, sometimes it's easier to demonstrate authority. It's more difficult to build relationships because it takes time and patience.

But when we follow Jesus' model of correction and avoid the temptation to criticize, we are better able to build long-lasting relationships and we increase our influence over those within our care. —*Tony Dungy*

### Go

1. How would you describe your style of discipline?

2. In what ways does correction differ from criticism?

3. What are some things that you can do to become less critical and more encouraging as a coach?

### Workout

Proverbs 3:11-12; Hebrews 12:11;
2 Timothy 3:16-17

### Overtime

*Father, thank You for loving me and helping me grow through correction. Help me to model Jesus' style of correction to those that I teach and influence. Amen.*

### Journal

**Journal**

# Making a Contribution

### Ready

*Then He said to them all, "If anyone wants to come with Me, he must deny himself, take up his cross daily, and follow Me."*

LUKE 9:23

### Set

In a recent survey, managers and employees were asked what aspects of their job were most important to them. The results uncovered that while the managers focused on things such as job security and benefits, the employees simply wanted to know that they were contributing— that what they were doing made a difference.

What is the first thing that we as athletes or coaches look for when we see the new team photograph? Ourselves, right? We all do. We are naturally selfish beings. Coaches might say, "There's no 'I' in 'team,'" but no matter how many times we reiterate this point, the "I" is always a problem. We fight a daily battle with selfishness, which of course affects how we contribute not only to our teams or businesses but also to our families—and even to our relationship with Christ.

Though it is human nature to be self-centered, it is also in our nature to genuinely want to make a contribution. However, the two are often in conflict with each other. This is why we should check our motives whenever we are in a position to give. Do we want to contribute based on the "I" or on the "team"? Is it about the "me" or about the "we"?

Jesus Christ was the only human who did not yield to selfish tendencies. He offered the greatest contribution humanity has ever known: the sacrifice of His life for our sins! In order to make a powerful impact for Christ and contribute our gifts to building His kingdom, we are called to follow His selfless example. Through His power in us, we can live out Jesus' words in Luke 9:23, denying ourselves in following Him. When we do, it will undoubtedly lead to the most significant contribution we'll ever make! —*Les Steckel*

### Go

1. Are your contributions for your sake, or for Christ and His body of believers?

2. When has another person put your needs before his or her own? How did you feel?

3. Are you on the side of the "me" or of the "we"?

## Workout

Proverbs 11:2; John 3:27-30;
Philippians 2:1-4; 1 Peter 5:1-7

## Overtime

*Lord, I pray that You would increase
in me as I decrease! Amen.*

## Journal

## Journal

# Fight the Good Fight

### Ready

*I have fought the good fight,*
*I have finished the race, I have kept the faith.*
2 TIMOTHY 4:7

### Set

When I'm recruiting players, one of the most important qualities I look for is fight. Fight is that one thing that serves as the axis for our team. If we do that, then we never have anything to be ashamed of. It's the one thing we can control. There will be things that will come and go: shooting percentages, adhering to a defensive scout, whatever it may be. But you *can* control how much effort you give and how hard you fight. It gives you the chance to be the best ever if you are talented, and it gives you a chance to compete even when you aren't as talented as your opponent.

Whether you're facing an illness or any sort of struggle that may come your way, fight is a way of life. That is also very true when it comes to our existence as Christians. In athletics, we coach our players to fight for loose balls or to fight through adversity on the playing field. But in the spiritual realm, we coach those within our influence to fight the good fight. We help prepare them to fight through adversities on this journey to our eternal life in heaven.

When you talk about gritting your teeth and standing your ground, maybe nowhere is it more important than in your daily Christian walk and in the moment-by-moment decisions. That means doing things that aren't always easy but what's necessary. That requires fight. That requires perseverance. And eventually, we will finish the race and be able to say, as the apostle Paul did, we have kept the faith. —*Sherri Coale*

### Go

1. In athletic terms, how would define the word "fight"?

2. Read 2 Timothy 4:6-8. What is the fight that Paul describes here?

3. How can you incorporate "fight" into the spiritual challenges and decisions you face daily?

### Workout

1 Corinthians 9:24-25; Colossians 3:17-24;
1 Timothy 6:12; 2 Timothy 4:6-8

### Overtime

*Father, thank You for giving me the strength to fight the good fight. Help me to stand against temptations and challenges that I face daily and stand up for my faith. Help me to have fight in my spiritual life. Amen.*

**Journal**

**Journal**

# 4

# Serve Others with Loyalty

### Ready

*No one has greater love than this, that someone would lay down his life for his friends.*
JOHN 15:13

### Set

In 1962, Bob Devaney came to Nebraska as the head coach. He was immediately successful his first several years. But then he had two years when the team went 6-4. Some of the fans were very disenchanted. They didn't necessarily want to fire Bob, but they were insistent that he fire some of the staff and make some changes. But Bob had no intentions of firing anyone in order to make his own situation more secure.

I was a member of that staff. I was about 30 years old and had a wife and three kids. His indication of loyalty meant a lot to me. When I took over for Bob as the head coach at Nebraska, I made sure to model and teach that same kind of loyalty to my coaching staff and our players.

On the other hand, disloyalty can be devastating to a team. When we are disloyal, we give in to self-serving attitudes and compromise our character. Essentially, disloyalty is a betrayal of friendship and a breaking of the trust. Once trust is broken, it's almost impossible to get it back. That's why loyalty is such a big deal.

In the Bible, we get an interesting example of loyalty through the life of Peter. As one of Jesus' disciples, Peter was bullish in his support of the Messiah, sometimes to the point of doing foolish things, like cutting off the ear of a Roman soldier. Although Peter denied Jesus at the time of His crucifixion, he ultimately became a powerful evangelist that helped establish the Church. Peter was loyal to Jesus, even to the death.

As coaches, one of the best ways we can serve our staff and our players is by showing them loyalty. In turn, loyalty then breeds trust, and there are perhaps no two greater tools for a team's success. —*Tom Osborne*

## Go

1. What are some obstacles to loyalty within a team?

2. What are some ways that you have tried to create a sense of trust and loyalty?

3. What are some other things you can do that might help root out disloyalty and distrust?

## Workout

Ruth 1:16-17; Proverbs 17:17; John 15:12-13

## Overtime

*Lord, teach me to understand the true value of loyalty. Help me build trust with my team and my brothers and sisters and Christ. Amen.*

### Journal

**Journal**

# 5

# P.U.S.H.

### Ready

*With every prayer and request, pray at all times
in the Spirit, and stay alert in this, with all
perseverance and intercession for all the saints.*

EPHESIANS 6:18

### Set

I will never forget watching Reggie Miller score
8 points in the last 32 seconds of a 1995 Eastern Conference NBA playoff game in Madison
Square Garden. Miller's never-say-die heroics
in the closing seconds gave the Indiana Pacers
a thrilling 2-point victory over the New York
Knicks. Throughout his 18-year career with the
Pacers, Miller was the picture of persistence. He
didn't make every clutch shot he took, but he
never stopped shooting them.

In an interview following his final NBA
game, he summed up his career by saying:

> I showed up each and every day to play.
> I played in 80 percent of my games,
> maybe more. I played hurt. You never
> knew when someone was coming to
> an Indiana Pacers basketball game
> for the first time . . . I always wanted

them to remember that they had an enjoyable experience when they saw the Indiana Pacers play.[1]

Just as Miller modeled persistence, so too do good coaches. Would a good coach ever tell her team to give up just because they were down by 10 points at halftime? Never! She would encourage her players to fight to the end, no matter how things looked at any point during the game. Athletes and coaches understand, perhaps better than most, the need for persistence when it comes to competition.

Can the same be said of us when it comes to prayer? Have we talked with God regularly and honestly? Have we prayed and persisted, even when it didn't look like victory was possible? Jesus said, "Keep searching, and you will find" (Matthew 7:7). We are to continue to come before God with our requests, even when it feels like nothing is happening.

I've seen popular bracelets with the acronym P.U.S.H. stitched on them: "Pray Until Something Happens." What a great reminder that we should never give up when it comes to making our requests known to a God who loves us and gave His Son that we might find Him!
—*Kathy Malone*

## Go

1. Do you have an attitude of perseverance when it comes to prayer?

2. What prayer have you given up on?

3. What is keeping you from picking up that prayer and bringing it back to the Father?

### Workout

Luke 18:1; Colossians 4:2; Philippians 4:6

### Overtime

*Lord, forgive me for giving up so easily when it comes to prayer. Teach me to persevere in prayer as Your unseen hand works in ways I can't see or understand. Draw me into Your presence today through Your Holy Spirit. Amen.*

### Journal

**Journal**

**Note**

1. Reggie Miller, interview with David Brenner and Conrad Brunner, "Farewell Questions and Answers." http://www.nba.com/pacers/news/ reggie_interview.html (accessed September 2005).

# 6

# Take a Break

### Ready

*Come to Me, all of you who are weary and
burdened, and I will give you rest.*

PSALM 37:7

### Set

When I was an assistant at Northern Illinois, I
was out recruiting with another coach named
Julie Brown. We were in St. Louis in the middle
of July and it had gotten to the point where
we were very tired. One Sunday morning, we
decided to read about the Sabbath in an at-
tempt to justify working that day. As we read
different Bible passages, it became very clear
that we could honor God or we could turn our
heads and continue on the recruiting trail. We
made a decision to take the day off, and from
that time forward, I've made rest a priority as
a coach.

The Sabbath isn't just a suggestion. It's a
command. When I started to schedule a Sabbath day into my week, that's when my career
really took off. It wasn't always on Sunday, but
it was always a day that was committed to rest.
Ever since, it's been a central point of balance
in my coaching career.

When you take time to rest, it's like the analogy of sharpening your saw. If your blade is dull, it takes longer to cut down the tree. But when you take time to sharpen your saw, the tree comes down quickly. Rest and solitude sharpen my saw. I can spend less time getting the same amount of work done. I can be more effective in working with people than if I'm tired or rundown.

It's okay to work really hard and get after it, but it's equally important to obey God and take that time of rest and solitude. In your obedience, He will give you the strength to work harder, better and smarter. —*Sue Semrau*

### Go

1. How often do you take time away? What does that time look like?

2. On a scale of 1-10, how effective do you feel after you've had targeted times of rest and solitude versus times when you've gone long periods of time without a break?

3. What steps can you take this week to plan a Sabbath day into your schedule?

### Workout

Exodus 20:8-11; Psalms 23; 37:7; Isaiah 58:13-14; Matthew 11:28-30; Mark 6:30-32

## Overtime

*Father, reveal to me the importance of giving You significant amounts of my time in rest and solitude. Give me the practical tools to implement a Sabbath day by which I can honor You and in turn receive strength, renewal and peace. Amen.*

## Journal

**Journal**

# 7

# Give God Control

### Ready

*Many plans are in a man's heart,
but the LORD's decree will prevail.*

PROVERBS 29:11

### Set

I'm a big believer that God is in charge of your life. I believe this because I've seen how God has directed my path, even though I might not have been aware at the time.

So many times I was in a certain place, like when I played for the Chicago Cubs, and I thought that I was going to play there the rest of my career. Then I went to Colorado and I thought I'd be there the rest of my career. And then I went to New York. In the beginning, New York was very difficult. I didn't understand why God put me there. But I realized over time that there is a reason for everything He does, and ultimately, He's in charge.

Many of the things that have happened in my life weren't situations that I would have chosen for myself. But God has put me where He has wanted me to go, not where I wanted to go.

Solomon wrote in Proverbs 29:11 that "Many plans are in a man's heart, but the LORD's decree will prevail." Fact is, God's plan is always much better than anything we could devise on our own. He always knows what is best for us. That's because He created us and knows us better than we know ourselves.

If you're not sure if you're in the right place at any stage as a coach, think about how your life would have been different if you hadn't stayed where God put you. Think about all of the people He's touched because of you. No matter what the circumstance, never forget that God is in control. —*Joe Girardi*

### Go

1. Have you ever been through a time when you questioned why God put you in a certain place?

2. How did God reveal to you that He was in control and you were exactly where He wanted you to be?

3. What is one area of your life you need to let God have complete control of?

### Workout

Jeremiah 29:11; Isaiah 55:8-11; Matthew 6:25-34; Romans 8:28

### Overtime

*Father, thank You for taking control of my life and placing me exactly where You want me to be. Help*

*me to see Your plan for my life and to trust You
with the future. Amen.*

**Journal**

**Journal**

# 8

# Priorities

## Ready

*Watch out and be on guard against
all greed, because one's life is not in
the abundance of his possessions.*

LUKE 12:15

## Set

At the beginning of every football season, Coach Tom Landry would give his players his priorities: God, family and football, in that order. By keeping these priorities, he avoided the madness and chaos that often consume a coach's life.

These priorities provide great wisdom for us as we seek balance in our lives. When we keep first things first, we honor God and others around us, which helps us avoid relational destruction. Sadly, though, many coaches become "life losers" because they put their sport first and everything else second. They measure their self-worth by what they accomplish on the athletic field and by the wins they attain. In the process, everything else suffers. Their families fall apart, and they feel empty because their soul is not being nourished by a relationship with God.

Jesus warns us against getting caught in this web of deception. In fact, He says that at the heart of this "accomplishment complex" is personal greed. For coaches, this translates as an attitude in which the only ambition is winning. But when we approach life in this way, everyone becomes a pawn in our game. If they can't produce for us, they become disposable. Family responsibilities become a nuisance, players who can't perform have little worth, and coaches who can't keep up are second-class citizens. This attitude produces a no-win season in God's eyes because it puts another god before the one true God, Jesus Christ.

Putting Jesus first means keeping Him at the center of all we do, remembering that we were at the center of why He came to Earth! By keeping Him first, we can't help but pursue excellence for His sake and keep our careers in proper perspective. Jesus wants to be our sole ambition—and when He is, our coaching will be better than ever! —*Al Schierbaum*

### Go

1. How does knowing that God loves you unconditionally shape your perspective?

2. What were Jesus' priorities?

3. What changes in your life can you make to reflect God's priorities?

## Workout

Psalm 127:1-5; Ecclesiastes 2:24-25;
Matthew 22:37-39; Galatians 5:16-26

## Overtime

*Gracious Father, turn my eyes away from the empty ambitions of this world so that I might see today the depths and riches of Your love in Christ Jesus!*

**Journal**

## Journal

# 9

# Coaching . . . Our Mission Field

### Ready

*Shepherd God's flock among you, not overseeing out of compulsion but freely, according to God's will; not for the money but eagerly; not lording it over those entrusted to you, but being examples to the flock. And when the chief Shepherd appears, you will receive the unfading crown of glory.*

1 PETER 5:2-4

### Set

Competition is an obvious part of the coaching life, resulting in either winning or losing. But God's Word reminds us not to get so caught up in the results that we forget to take care of the flock—the athletes—who have been put under our watch.

Of course, we all want to win. Yet if we forget that we're really working toward an imperishable crown (as Paul writes in 1 Corinthians 9:25), then we've lost sight of why we're coaching in the first place. In other words, just as we live our lives to please the Good Shepherd, so too should we coach our players with the same goal. In the process, we'll serve as examples to the sheep.

The Lord has given us our "mission field," and He cares more about how we take care of the people He has entrusted to us than He does about our win-loss record. This is why Peter provides us with guidelines from the verses above on how to serve our athletes. We are to guide the flock (team) not by coercion or constraint, but willingly; not dishonorably, motivated by the advantages and profits, but eagerly and cheerfully; not with intimidation, but by being an example to them. And when the Chief Shepherd, Jesus Christ, appears again, we will win the unfading crown of glory!

This is our hope. Until then, God is able to help us accomplish our goal every day, through not only our words but also our actions, as He cares for our players through us! —*Sue Ramsey*

### Go

1. Does your coaching style reflect the shepherding characteristics described by Peter?

2. What creative ways could you care for your athletes and thereby please Christ?

3. When you honestly assess your motives, do you seek advantages and profits, or do you work eagerly and cheerfully? Does this area of your coaching need adjusting?

## Workout

Isaiah 40:11; John 10:11-15;
1 Corinthians 9:24-27

## Overtime

*Lord, may our focus, our top priority, for our
athletes be based on the things above, the eternal
purpose: Your glory! In Christ's name, amen.*

### Journal

**Journal**

# 10

# Be Adaptable

### Ready

*I know both how to have a little, and I know how
to have a lot. In any and all circumstances I have
learned the secret of being content—whether well
fed or hungry, whether in abundance or in need.*

PHILIPPIANS 4:12

### Set

As the head coach at St. John's University, I was
on top of the world. It was 2003 and we had
just won the NIT, I had co-authored a book,
and I had made an appearance in a feature
film. But a few months later, I was fired and
completely out of coaching. I thought I would
never coach again.

So my wife and I moved to Florida where we
got plugged into a great church and the Lord
really grabbed hold of my heart. After working
some for ESPN, I was blessed with the opportunity to become the head coach at Florida Atlantic University. It was a big adjustment. When
you coach at a smaller program like FAU, you
have recruit kids that have usually stayed below
the radar. You have to be patient. You have to
give them time to mature as young men and
as athlete.

The experience has taught me so much about adaptability and flexibility. Situations are always changing and if you can't adjust, then the chances of you overcoming are not going to be there.

The apostle Paul provides us with one of the Bible's best examples of adaptability. He was preaching to the poor and destitute one moment and going head to head with dignitaries and rulers the next. Paul became all things to all people in order to reach them all for the sake of the eternal Kingdom.

Following God's path can take you down a road that will wind a lot, and it will take as much time as God wants it to take. Once you realize that you're on His watch, you'll see that He is teaching you patience and helping you develop the ability to adapt to any circumstance that you might face as a leader. —*Mike Jarvis*

### Go

1. In the past, how well have you adapted to change?

2. How has God used that time of change to train and prepare you for something greater?

3. How might being more adaptable help you follow God's path for your life?

### Workout

1 Corinthians 9:19-23; 2 Timothy 4:2-5

### Overtime

*Father, thank You for being in control of my life. Thank You for walking with me through the long and winding road. Help me to be adaptable to Your plan and to trust You through the changes. Amen.*

**Journal**

**Journal**

# 11

# Operate in Truth

### Ready

*You will know the truth,
and the truth will set you free.*
JOHN 8:32

### Set

One year when I was coaching at the University of Wisconsin, I instituted a no-drinking policy after several girls showed up to a Saturday morning practice smelling like a brewery. This was not normal for me, but I was so upset that I had them all sign a piece of paper stating they would not drink during the season or they would be suspended from the team.

We were playing in the WNIT when I received an email from a season ticket holder who had seen seven of my players out drinking at a bar. The next day, I asked for those seven players to confess. They all told me the truth and I suspended them. Somehow, we managed to win our next game despite half of our team sitting out.

Who you are as a coach must revolve around truth. It can't be based on appearances. Otherwise, your foundation won't be able to withstand the tests that are going to come your way. In my story, telling the truth came in the form of tough love. When my players failed to meet certain expectations, I held firm to my disciplinary action despite the consequences.

Jesus was the ultimate purveyor of truth. He dealt with what was on the inside. He looked at the heart. When Jesus met the Samaritan woman at the well, He accepted her for who she was. He gently called out her sin but then lovingly led her down a road of redemption. It was the truth that set her free, even though it was probably not an easy thing to hear.

Truthfulness will bring respect. Your players and coaches will know what they're going to get from you when you operate in truth. They may not always like you or sometimes they may get angry with you, but they will respect you because they will know that you are always going to tell them the truth. —*Jane Albright*

### Go

1. In what areas of your life do you struggle with truth?

2. How do you deal with untruthfulness from those you're leading?

3. What are some ways you can begin to create an environment that fosters reciprocal truth amongst your team or group?

## Workout

Job 27:4-6; Proverbs 12:19; Matthew 4:1-26; Ephesians 4:15

## Overtime

*Father, search my heart and shine the spotlight on any untruthfulness that is hidden there. Give me the grace to rid myself of any dishonest motives and fill me with Your unconditional love. Help me model truth to those in my care so that they might lead a greater life of integrity. Amen.*

**Journal**

**Journal**

# 12

# Dreams

### Ready

*Now to Him who is able to do above and beyond all that we ask or think—according to the power that works in you—to Him be glory in the church and in Christ Jesus to all generations, forever and ever.*

EPHESIANS 3:20-21

### Set

Every year I look at my team's schedule of games during preseason and start to calculate wins and losses. One game I'm certain we'll win; another we probably won't; still another will be a toss-up. Though each season is filled with uncertainty and challenges, most coaches I know still dream about championships and MVP awards. What's exciting to me is that God can do immeasurably more than all of these expectations combined.

In the apostle Paul's letter to his friends in Ephesus, he reminds them that God's ability far surpasses their dreams. According to the power that He works in those who believe, God is willing to go above and beyond what humans can imagine. In other words, God's reality is even bigger than anything we could dream!

This means that God's plans for each of us are even greater than any we could dream of on our own, and He proves that to us in the person of Jesus Christ. Who could have imagined that a perfect God would provide a way for imperfect people like us to come into His presence? But He did just that when Jesus took the penalty for our sins on the cross, becoming the bridge to a daily relationship with the Almighty! And because of His faithful provision of grace, we can absolutely trust God to make provision for our lives in ways that we can't even conceive. He is able to do immeasurably more than all we even know to ask or imagine. That's how great God's power is in our lives. His reality is bigger than our dreams!

Whatever challenges we as coaches face today, we can face them with the confidence that comes from God when we step into the reality of His plans, knowing that His life and power eclipse our wildest dreams! —*Roger Lipe*

### Go

1. What are your dreams for your team, your family and your personal life?

2. Is your influence for Christ limited by the size of your dreams?

3. What are your God-sized dreams?

## Workout

1 Kings 3:7-14; John 14:12-14;
Ephesians 3:14-20

## Overtime

*Lord, thank You that Your dreams for me are greater than any I could imagine on my own. In Jesus Christ, amen.*

### Journal

Journal

# 13

# Use Your Influence

### Ready

*Let your light shine before men, so that
they may see your good works and give
glory to your Father in heaven.*

MATTHEW 5:16

### Set

As a baseball manager, I'm not just here to serve
my players and my coaches. I'm here to serve
God in whatever capacity He needs to use me
each and every day. And as a Christ follower
in the public eye, it's my job to live out my
faith and use my platform to influence those
around me.

There are a lot of tools we have available to
us to help share the gospel with others, but
nothing will speak louder than our actions. It's
good to be vocal, but if you don't back that
up with action, those words will ring hollow.
You can pick up the paper every day and read
about people who talk about doing right but
who don't do right. Our actions will always
speak louder than our words.

But when you use your platform to influence others for the Kingdom, you'd better be
ready for the criticism. When I was managing

the Colorado Rockies, disapproving members of the media and other outside groups consistently challenged the team's executives.

For many years, I didn't stand for anything. So now is my time to stand for something. I believe in what I stand for with all my heart. That's what's important to me. I'm not doing this to get applause or to get a good rating in a Gallup poll and find out who agrees with what I'm doing. That's insignificant. The only thing that matters is eternity.

As coaches, we have great influence on players, other coaches and fans. No matter how big or small our platforms might be, there's no better time than now to use that influence to bring glory to our Father in heaven. —*Clint Hurdle*

### Go

1. How would you describe your circle of influence?

2. What are some challenges that make it difficult for you to maximize your platform for the sake of the Kingdom?

3. What are some things that you can do today that will help you shine your light even brighter?

### Workout

Isaiah 6:8; Matthew 5:3-16; 28:19-20;
1 Peter 3:16

## Overtime

*Lord, give me the courage to shine my light into every part of my world. Help me follow Your Spirit as I endeavor to share the truth of the gospel with those in my circle of influence. Amen.*

### Journal

**Journal**

# 14

# A New Heart

### Ready

*From now on, then, we do not know anyone in a purely human way. Even if we have known Christ in a purely human way, yet now we no longer know Him like that. Therefore if anyone is in Christ, there is a new creation; old things have passed away, and look, new things have come.*

2 CORINTHIANS 5:16-17

### Set

In our pregame talks, we tell our players to "play with heart!" and encourage them to perform their best. The more our players develop such a vision, the deeper their commitment to the sport becomes. This is exactly what Jesus wants from us. He wants to develop a heart in us that will commit to knowing Him in a deeper, more intimate way. As David said in Psalm 51:10, "God, create a clean heart for me and renew a steadfast spirit within me." As we develop this kind of heart, others will notice.

For years, I believed in who God was, but I did not have a relationship with Him. The only relationship I thought that I could count on was my relationship with my grandparents. Then the Lord brought a friend into my life to "coach" me into wanting a relationship with Him. She cared enough about me to show me her heart. As a result, I was so drawn to Jesus that I surrendered and made Him more than my Savior—He became the Lord of my life. As I learned to trust Him and accept His grace and compassion, all of my relationships changed. So did my coaching!

As coaches who follow Christ, we can pour out to others what He has poured into us. He'll restore and rejuvenate our relationships as He continues to change our hearts. And as we rest in Him and continue to be transformed into His likeness, the peace, hope and joy we experience with Him will show our players what it really means to play with heart! —*Lisa Phillips*

### Go

1. How would you describe your team's heart? Your heart?

2. Think of those people whom God put in your life to model heart and faith. How could you now encourage them?

3. In what ways has your life become new since acknowledging Jesus as Lord?

### Workout

Psalm 51; Matthew 22:37-40; Ephesians 3:19

## Overtime

*Lord, I pray as David prayed that You would create in me a clean heart for Your purposes. Amen.*

### Journal

**Journal**

**15**

# Troubled?

### Ready

*Your heart must not be troubled.*
*Believe in God; believe also in Me.*
JOHN 14:1

### Set

Trouble and being troubled are two completely different things. Trouble is being down by a run, nobody on base, with two outs in the bottom of the ninth and our worst hitter coming to the plate. Being troubled is having no strategy for this scenario and not being prepared to accept the possible consequences that are about to come.

As coaches, there will be many times when we will have to declare to our team, "Don't worry, everything will be okay." We might even complete our short speech with the same words that Jesus did: "Believe in me." But if we haven't demonstrated believability to our players, these words will have absolutely no value. Without having the same credibility that Jesus had, our words will be like wisps of air.

In John 14:1, Jesus told His disciples, "Your heart must not be troubled. Believe in God; believe also in Me." Through His words, Christ offered His followers comfort for the difficult days ahead. He knew that they were about to face some major trouble—serious persecution and, for some, even death. Jesus knew that trouble was coming for Him and for His followers, but He didn't want them to be troubled while facing it. And He doesn't want us to be troubled either.

As coaches, we need to aim high in becoming trustworthy to help our student athletes reach their potential. If our players can't trust us, then why should they follow us? Of course, God is the only one worthy of total trust—confirmed through Christ's willing sacrifice on the cross—but His new life inside us can make us trustworthy as well.

He invites us in the midst of any trouble that we are experiencing to bring our troubled hearts to our trustworthy God. Because even when our hearts are troubled, the ultimate remedy is still the same—totally trusting the Lord! —*Clay Elliot*

### Go

1. How have you faced a troubled situation?

2. Are your words like wisps of air to your team, or are they credible and valued?

3. What in the past has helped you face trouble?

## Workout

2 Samuel 24:10; Luke 24:36-49; John 14:27-31

## Overtime

*Lord, if trouble comes today, help me to come to You, believing that You will work it out according to Your good purposes! Thank You in Christ's name, amen.*

## Journal

## Journal

# 16

# Our Identity in Christ

### Ready

*Since, then, you have been raised with Christ, set your hearts on things above, where Christ is seated at the right hand of God. Set your mind on things above, not on earthly things.*

COLOSSIANS 3:1-2, *NIV*

### Set

As coaches, whenever we are asked, "How are you?" we often reply in terms of our team: "We struggled early but regrouped late in the season."

Unfortunately, it's far too easy for us as coaches to become consumed with our team's performance. When we allow this to happen, who we are can get lost amid the pressure to win. Learning to separate athletic expectations from our true identity in Christ is an ongoing and significant challenge.

As followers of Christ, we are not to lose sight of what matters most in this life. In Paul's letter to the Christians in the city of Colossae, he voiced concerns about the distractions of the time and their inherent dangers. He issued a warning to the Colossians (and to us) to pay attention and to be on guard because this world can be a captivating place.

Paul knew that this world's temporal rewards beckon with a fierce and determined strength. And just as the false teachings were attractive to the misguided Colossians, so too can a winning record be equally alluring to a coach!

If we become ensnared by the rewards and attention inherent in success, we make ourselves vulnerable to the idolatrous practices that Paul warned against. Focusing our lives on anything but those "things above" is a recipe for failure. We will continually be disappointed and feel a loss of hope and will look to the next season or next recruit to fulfill us.

Paul is clear: Nothing of human design should become the focal point in our lives, even something as seemingly noble as leading a team to a successful season. Anything that stands in the way of our relationship with Christ keeps us from fully surrendering our hearts and minds to Him. And only He can satisfy our longings! —*Cheryl Baird*

### Go

1. Can you separate who you are in Christ from your team's performance?

2. What will it take for you to set your mind on "things above"?

3. What does it mean for you to surrender your team to God?

## Workout

Psalm 26:2-3; Philippians 3:7-20;
Colossians 2:8

## Overtime

*God, I want to find my whole identity in You!
Please help me release the desire to replace You
with anything that is of this world. Amen.*

## Journal

**Journal**

# 17

# Practice, Practice!

### Ready

*Do what you have learned and received
and heard and seen in me, and the God
of peace will be with you.*
PHILIPPIANS 4:9

### Set

We've all said it: The secret to success is practice, practice, practice. Sometimes we'll put the word "perfect" in front of all of those "practices" to nail down an even more effective plan. We all know that without practice we'll never reach the level of play that we desire.

When I was in high school, I trusted my coaches completely, so I practiced whatever they told me to. I desired success, which helped me to listen to them and heed their advice. In the same way, when we read that Paul urges us to "do what you have learned and received and heard and seen in me," we would be wise to heed his advice. A quick scan of the context reveals some of what Paul would want us to put into practice:

- Philippians 4:4—We should rejoice in the Lord.

- Philippians 4:5—Our gentleness should be evident (*NIV*).

- Philippians 4:6—We should pray about everything.

- Philippians 4:8—We should think about the good stuff.

As coaches, we can integrate these four ideas daily by rejoicing not just in winning but in practice or tough defeats; leading our players with gentleness as the Lord leads us; praying for our players and for every decision, from game plans to practice sessions; and filling our minds by meditating on God's goodness and promises.

Only when we put these Christlike attributes into practice with His help will we have the reserves to see the good when difficult circumstances arise. As we do, our faith in Him will be deepened and our Christian lives will become more authentic. In other words, we'll learn more of what it means to be "real" coaches. We'll become more like the people that God always intended us to be through Jesus Christ our Lord as we practice, practice, practice with Him! —*Clay Elliot*

### Go

1. What are the attributes of a "real" coach?

2. How do those characteristics compare with your coaching style?

3. What are some things that you could put into practice with God's help?

### Workout

Psalm 111:1-10; Philippians 4:1-9;
1 Timothy 4:11-16

### Overtime

*Thank You, Lord, that You hear my prayers and fill me with Your joy and gentleness. I ask for Your wisdom today as I reflect Your glory and grace to each person that You bring across my path. Amen.*

### Journal

**Journal**

# 18

# Take Time To Teach

### Ready

*Make yourself an example of good works with
integrity and dignity in your teaching.*

TITUS 2:7

### Set

I believe that teaching is a prerequisite for all
great coaches, but teaching is not something
that you just try to do. It's a part of who you
are. If you're a great coach, you're always teaching. Great coaches teach and sometimes they
don't even know that they're teaching.

I've been blessed with many great teachers
in my life. My first teacher was my mom. I
have also received great teaching from Baylor
head football coach Grant Teaff, his assistant
Corky Nelson, and NFL coach Buddy Ryan. I
was also deeply impacted by my college English teacher Ann Miller, and both my father
and my wife.

Unfortunately, there are so few teachers today because people don't have time. And because of that, the students don't think they're
important enough. As the teaching component
in our society wanes, we are in danger of losing
this generation.

But once you are willing to step up and be a teacher who is willing to mentor others, you must also take time to learn. For me, that means learning everything I can about Jesus Christ, learning everything there is to know about being a great husband and a great dad, and learning everything there is to know about coaching.

As I learn more about Christ, I realize that there is no teacher that compares to Him. The greatest lessons I've learned about teaching have come from just reading about His life. The words He said challenge me every day. He spoke the truth and had great wisdom in how He approached each individual.

Great coaches are great teachers. And the opportunity we have to pour into the lives of young men and women is an exciting but humbling call. Take time to learn. Take time to teach. The impact you have on others will be measured by eternal standards. —*Mike Singletary*

## Go

1. What teachers have had the greatest influence in your life? What did you learn from them?

2. In what ways can you improve your knowledge and wisdom in order to be a better teacher?

3. Who are some people in your circle of influence that you can begin teaching today?

## Workout

Psalm 32:8; Proverbs 22:6;
Hebrews 5:12; Titus 2

## Overtime

*Father, give me the heart of a teacher. Help me to
see how I might influence those around me by
pouring into them the knowledge and wisdom
other teachers have poured into my life. Amen.*

## Journal

**Journal**

# 19

# Pressure Release

### Ready

*To the weak I became weak, in order to win the weak. I have become all things to all people, so that I may by all means save some. Now I do all this because of the gospel, so that I may become a partner in its benefits.*

1 CORINTHIANS 9:22-23

### Set

We entered summer league basketball with a young team. Our inexperienced guards struggled to get our offense working, especially against a high-pressure, man-to-man defense.

One day in practice, I tried a new strategy. I taught my players several pressure-release, back-door plays that changed our focus and took advantage of the defense. I told them that we would invite the pressure so that we could cut and score lay-ups. My players were skeptical.

In the next game, when the defense was zealous and our guards wide-eyed, I called a time-out to remind the team what we'd learned. Back on the court, still afraid, my players decided to try to execute the play. Our wing came toward the sideline, and then cut to the basket. Our point guard passed to her and she scored! The way the team celebrated, you'd have thought we had won a championship!

Sometimes, the toughest defenses that coaches face are the walls our players put up. We try to love and care for them, but they're not so sure of us. They ignore instruction from us on the court or field, cross their arms, avoid eye contact and dare us to connect with them. The harder we try, the tougher their defenses become. As coaches of such players, we need to master the backdoor play.

Paul understood this and "became all things to all people . . . [to] save some." Because God came to Earth as a man to reach us, He can help us find ways to release the pressure that our players might feel.

As we begin to understand how to reach our players in creative, back-door ways, the defenses will come down, and we can speak into their hearts the love of Christ! —*Debbie Haliday*

### Go

1. Do you expect your players to adjust to you, or do you sometimes adjust to them?

2. Do some players resist your coaching? Do you pray for them?

3. What are some specific back-door strategies that you could add to your team's routine to help them get to know you better and trust you more?

## Workout
Isaiah 61; John 15:9-17; Acts 17:22-31

## Overtime
*Father, please give me the creativity and energy
I need to coach this generation of athletes for
Your sake. In Jesus' name, amen.*

## Journal

**Journal**

# 20

# The Plan

### Ready

*For I know the plans I have for you—[this is]*
*the Lord's declaration—plans for [your] welfare,*
*not for disaster, to give you a future and a hope.*
*You will call to Me and come and pray*
*to Me, and I will listen to you.*
JEREMIAH 29:11-12

### Set

As a football coach at both the college and high school levels, it seemed like I was always making plans. I would spend hours watching films and charting out an opposing team's offensive tendencies. I would then try to come up with a strategy to stop their offense. When the season was over, I would start preparing to improve our team in the off-season. Whether it was coming up with a plan to recruit the best high school players or organizing an off-season weight-lifting program, it seemed as if I was always planning for something.

The big thing with plans is that we have to trust they will work. We might start out with a goal, come up with a strategy to attain it, and then trust that our hard work will pay off. But there is one catch: No plan of ours ever works exactly the way it did on paper! Only one plan has ever come out as it was intended, and that is God's!

The prophet Jeremiah wrote that God's declaration to us involves a plan for our welfare, to care for us and to provide for us the gift of hope each day of our earthly lives. In the person of Jesus Christ, God's promise has been fulfilled! For it is through the gospel of Christ—that is, the good news of His life, death and resurrection—that we are saved from disaster and given a future that is anchored in His marvelous love. His plan has always been to bring us into a personal relationship with Him—not to have us fulfill a set of goals and strategies! By seeking God's presence, we can always be confident that He has a plan. —*Michael Hill*

### Go

1. How are you actively seeking God in your life?

2. In what area of your life are you having problems trusting God?

3. What steps can you take to trust in God's purposes for your life?

### Workout

Joshua 1:9; Psalm 20:7; Proverbs 3:5; 16:20; 1 Peter 2:6

## Overtime

*Lord, today when I'm tempted to pursue my own strategy or agenda, draw me close to You so that Your Kingdom purposes might be fulfilled in me! Amen.*

**Journal**

**Journal**

# 21

# Process Over Product

### Ready

*Do you not know that the runners in a stadium all race, but only one receives the prize? Run in such a way that you may win. Now everyone who competes exercises self-control in everything. However, they do it to receive a perishable crown; but we an imperishable one.*

1 CORINTHIANS 9:24-25

### Set

Like most high school coaches, I had a goal to some day help an athlete win a state championship. As a former 800-meter runner, I wanted to help an athlete win that exact event. In my first season as a high school distance coach, achieving this goal became a possibility when one of my runners made it to the finals of the 800-meter at the state meet. But it was there that God taught me a valuable lesson.

I had expected to be at the finals in five or ten years, not in my very first year. But I also didn't expect to feel the emptiness that I felt as I watched my runner compete. I wondered if this was what coaching was all about. I remembered how much time had gone into training this one athlete as well as the time spent training my other athletes. I weighed that against how much time I'd committed to these athletes' personal and spiritual growth and quickly realized that I'd fallen into the trap that many coaches fall into: I'd made the product—the goal of winning—a higher priority than the process of shaping lives.

That day, I learned two things: (1) God is more concerned with how things are accomplished than with what is accomplished; and (2) God doesn't care about numbers as much as He cares about hearts—and He proved this to all humankind when He sent His only Son to Earth to take our sins to the cross.

As the gun went off that day, I decided that no matter the outcome, I would from that time forward be as much or more concerned with the spiritual training of my athletes than I was with their physical training! —*Toby C. Schwartz*

### Go

1. Are you more concerned with winning than you are with the growth of your athletes?

2. What goals do you consider most important?

3. Does the process drive the goals, or do the goals drive the process?

## Workout

Ezekiel 11:17-21; Matthew 23:23-28;
Luke 16:14-18

## Overtime

*Thank You, Lord, that You've given me the
privilege of caring for my athletes today. Help
me to show them the imperishable crown that
Jesus Christ offers to us! Amen.*

## Journal

**Journal**

# 22

# Recharging

### Ready

*Now faith is the reality of what is hoped for,*
*the proof of what is not seen.*

HEBREWS 11:1

### Set

As the head women's basketball coach at the same institution for 26 years, I had just completed a rewarding season. We had a great group of athletes who played their hearts out, got along well and won games. There were many magical moments during the season, and no one wanted it to be over. But all good things must come to an end.

Like many coaches, I went through a period of letdown in which I needed to recharge for the next season. Though we'd just finished one season, a new one was around the corner. Thankfully, I had learned years before that what I enjoyed most about coaching was the process of preparing for "what is not seen." So even though I didn't know what tomorrow or the next season would bring, which recruits we'd need, or whether those recruits would blend well with the veterans, I knew that the unknowns at the end of a season didn't have to be unnerving. Instead, they could be exciting—if I had faith!

That's why I'm encouraged that "faith is the reality of what is hoped for." It energizes us. As coaches, we don't have to rely on ourselves, our players or our records. Instead, because Christ gave up His control by going to the cross for our sake, we can give up control and rely on Him. His peace is "the proof of what is not seen," regardless of the circumstances.

It quiets me to know that God is in control and that, win or lose, Christ has given me the faith to tackle another season and the hope that the best is yet to come! As we prepare for the unknowns of the next season (or even the next contest), we can rest in the assurance that Christ has filled us with His Holy Spirit, offering us hope for eternity and recharging us along the way! —*Susan Johnson*

### Go

1. How do you recharge between each season?

2. Do the unknowns of the future unnerve you or give you hope?

3. Has your faith in Christ enabled you to share an optimistic attitude with those around you?

### Workout

Jeremiah 14:22; Luke 12:22-31; Romans 12:12

## Overtime

*Lord, increase my faith in You today. Thank You for the gift of peace in Jesus Christ. Amen.*

### Journal

**Journal**

# 23

# What Will You Be Remembered For?

## Ready

*Therefore, fear the Lord and worship Him in sincerity and truth. Get rid of the gods your ancestors worshiped beyond the Euphrates River and in Egypt, and worship the Lord.*

JOSHUA 24:14

## Set

Not long ago, I stopped in a nearby town for coffee. When I went to wash my hands, I noticed the shiny new hand dryer on the restroom wall with the words "Feel the Power" printed on it.

I pushed the button and got a blast of hot air! It was like one of those huge dryers from the car wash had been compacted into a tiny hand dryer. Now, whenever someone mentions that town, I think of that hand dryer, a silly reminder of my experience there!

Sometimes I wonder how I'll be remembered as a coach. When someone mentions my coaching career, will they note the wins and losses, the calls I made or failed to make? Or will they remember how I served and acted as a coach?

When people talk about Joshua, the first thing I remember is that he chose to serve the Lord when he could have pursued any other way to live. Joshua's life and leadership clearly reflected what he believed and whom he followed: God. He knew that humans are made to worship and that if we do not worship the one true God, we will worship another.

Thankfully, God sent His Son, Jesus Christ, to lead us to Himself and then gave us His Holy Spirit to fill us with the power we need to believe! When we submit ourselves to His lordship, our lives will reflect His contagious love and selfless power.

People might never know just who is behind our actions, but they will remember that something about our lives was different! They might forget records and scores, but they will not forget our Christlike actions. —*Rex Stump*

### Go

1. Which do you remember most: past scores, records or people?

2. What do you remember about one of your coaches or teammates?

3. How do you want to be remembered?

### Workout

Psalm 112; Ecclesiastes 2; Ezekiel 18:21-32; Ephesians 1:17-20

## Overtime

*Lord, thank You that Your resurrection power
is working in me to create a life that reminds
others of You! Amen.*

### Journal

**Journal**

# 24

# Consumed by a Desire to Serve

### Ready

*Based on the gift they have received, everyone should use it to serve others, as good managers of the varied grace of God. If anyone speaks, his speech should be like the oracles of God; if anyone serves, his service should be from the strength God provides, so that in everything God may be glorified through Jesus Christ. To Him belong the glory and the power forever and ever. Amen.*

1 PETER 4:10-11

### Set

As Christian competitors, we realize that God has called us to serve. But do we understand that we should be consumed to serve? Is there a consuming fire that burns in us to serve others around us who are hurting and to help those who need to experience the love of Christ through us?

We serve because the ultimate purpose of serving is to glorify Christ. Rick Warren said, "We serve God by serving others. The world defines greatness in terms of power, possessions, prestige, and position. In our self-serving culture with its me-first mentality, acting like a servant is not a popular concept."[1] In the athletic world, everyone struggles to some degree with the me-first mentality. We buy into the lie that we are better than others because of our giftedness in athletics. So, are we consumed with self or consumed with serving?

When serving, we need to have intentionality (plan it!), intensity (seize it!) and intimacy (feel it!). The passion for serving must come from the heart. Samuel Chadwick said it best: "Spirit filled souls are ablaze for God. They love with a love that glows. They serve with a faith that kindles. They serve with a devotion that consumes. They hate sin with fierceness that burns. They rejoice with a joy that radiates. Love is perfected in the fire of God."[2]

On and off the field of competition, we need to be radical about serving. Can you imagine if thousands of coaches and athletes across the country got passionate about serving their teams? Why shouldn't that revolution begin with you? —*Dan Britton*

### Go

1. Why is it hard to be passionate about serving? What gets in the way?

2. What part of your life reflects the me-first mentality? Identify it, confess it, and ask for forgiveness.

3. Will you be one of the thousands who are passionate about serving?

If so, what is one practical way you
can serve your team today?

## Workout

Jude 1:24-25

## Overtime

*Jesus, this serving thing is hard. I struggle daily
with the me-first mentality. I confess my selfishness
before You. Help me to see with spiritual eyes
the ways I can serve my team. I want to be one
who is consumed to serve. Amen.*

## Journal

**Journal**

### Notes

1. Rick Warren, *The Purpose-Driven Life: What on Earth Am I Here For?* (Grand Rapids, MI: Zondervan Publishing House), Day 33.
2. Samuel Chadwick, quoted on "WatchCry Quotes: Provoking Thoughts on Prayer, Revival and Missions," Revival Resource Center. http://www.watch word.org/fire_from _the_altar_of_prayer.htm (accessed October 2005).

# 25

# An Attitude of Gratitude

### Ready

*Rejoice always! Pray constantly.*
*Give thanks in everything, for this is*
*God's will for you in Christ Jesus.*
1 THESSALONIANS 5:16-18

### Set

If you were to list the qualities of the people you most admire, a thankful attitude would probably be at the top of the list. Attitude will make or break a person. In his book *Developing the Leader Within You*, John Maxwell says this concerning attitude:

> The disposition of a leader is important because it will influence the way the followers think and feel. Great leaders understand that the right attitude will set the right atmosphere, which enables the right responses from others.[1]

Attitude is always a choice. You may not be able to control circumstances, but you can control how you react to those circumstances.

Knowing that God is in control should make a difference in one's attitude. In fact, 1 Thessalonians 5:16-18 implies that our trust in God is directly linked to our attitude. One of the most difficult disciplines in life is the discipline of thankfulness—taking time to thank God for the team, children and spouse He has given you; taking time to count your blessings and adjust your attitude.

Paying bills used to be a pain in my side. When I would finish, I would be like an angry bear. (Can you relate? Most coaches can identify with the bumper sticker that reads "My take-home pay won't even take me home!") Interest, taxes and high costs for services all made me angry. Then, one day as I was writing out the checks, the Lord spoke to my heart about being thankful that He had provided the income to pay those bills. Since that day, as I write each check, I have thanked God for His provision, and I am no longer like an angry bear when I finish. —*Al Schierbaum*

### Go

1. What are some blessings that God has given to you in the past year?

2. What attitudes bring glory to God?

3. How does your attitude create the right atmosphere for your team?

## Workout

Psalm 46:10; Matthew 5:14-16;
Philippians 4:6-7; 1 Thessalonians 5:12-22

## Overtime

*Father, thank You for the way You love me
and want Your best for me. Thank You for
the peace that surpasses all understanding.*

## Journal

**Journal**

**Note**
1. John C. Maxwell, *Developing the Leader Within You* (Nashville, TN: Thomas Nelson Business, 2000), p. 98.

# God's Grace

### Ready

*My soul, praise the Lord, and do not forget all
His benefits. He forgives all your sin; He heals
all your diseases. He redeems your life from
the Pit; He crowns you with faithful love and
compassion. He satisfies you with goodness;
your youth is renewed like the eagle.*

PSALM 103:2-5

### Set

If we were to count on our hands the number
of times someone has let us down or the number of times we've disappointed someone else,
we'd definitely run out of fingers! As humans,
we fail all the time, whether it be in our relationships, careers or daily disciplines. In fact,
our life on Earth seems full of opportunities
to learn from our mistakes. So it's a good thing
that we have promises like Psalm 103:12: "As
far as the east is from the west, so far has He
removed our transgressions from us."

But an incredible thing happens when we
begin to see ourselves through the eyes of our
heavenly Father. No matter what mistakes we
make, no matter the pain or regret we might
feel, in God's eyes we shine brightly. How is

it possible that He would see us as righteous and dearly loved? As the old hymn "Before the Throne of God Above" puts it:

> Because the sinless Savior died, my sinful soul is counted free! For God the Just is satisfied, to look on Him and pardon me.[1]

Because of the perfect life of Jesus Christ on Earth, we can move beyond those feelings of inadequacy and shame to partake of His transforming grace! His presence in our daily lives redeems us, rescues us from the pit and showers us with love and compassion. Yes, He satisfies our desires with wonderful things! And no matter where we've been or what we've done, God continually invites us to Himself so that He can restore us and use us for His purposes—especially when we see ourselves through His eyes of grace! —*Danny Burns*

### Go

1. What causes you to be ashamed of your actions?

2. Do you realize that you are loved and forgiven?

3. What can you do to become the bright creation God sees?

### Workout

Micah 7:18-19; Luke 15:1-7;
Romans 5:1-11; 1 John 3:1-3

### Overtime

*Lord God, change my heart today so that I might be confident of Your love, and fill my mind with thoughts of Your grace so that others might also know You! In Christ's name, amen.*

### Journal

**Journal**

**Note**
1. Charitie L. Bancroft, "Before the Throne of God Above." http://www.cyberhymnal.org/htm/b/e/beforetg.htm (accessed September 2005).

# Self-Sacrifice

### Ready

*Peter began to tell Him, "Look, we have
left everything and followed You."*

MARK 10:28

### Set

When most sport seasons end, numbers get
crunched. As coaches, it's easy for us to get
caught up in this number crunching, especially
as the media highlights our career wins, the titles we've won and the number of "Coach of
the Year" awards we've received.

But any true coach knows that records
are not what are important. Having the opportunity to work with athletes and make a
difference in their lives is what is important.
Coaches, like players, make a lot of sacrifices
to develop winning teams, but most will tell
you that those sacrifices and successes are for
the athletes—for the joy of watching players
mature and grow.

In the Christian life, we make sacrifices as
well. Instead of sitting in front of the television
after a long day, we volunteer for church com-
mittees, sing in the choir, or work in the soup
kitchen. What motivates us to do these things?

If it is to build up a store of good deeds, then we're more concerned with building a record as Christians than with honoring Christ. In other words, our "sacrificial" serving isn't really serving anyone but ourselves.

In his book *My Utmost for His Highest*, Oswald Chambers asks:

> Have you ever been driven to do something for God not because you felt that it was useful or your duty to do so, or that there was anything in it for you, but simply because you love Him?[1]

As a Christian, I am called to serve Christ because I love Him, not because I need to earn His love. In fact, there is nothing that I could do to earn His love—Christ already paid the price for that love when He died on the cross!

We are not called to serve Christ for personal gain; for, like Peter, we have left everything to follow Jesus! For Christian coaches, genuine love for our athletes motivates a selfless commitment to them. Winning takes care of itself.
—*Donna Miller*

## Go

1. Are you more concerned about your players' successes, as individuals and as athletes, than you are about your own coaching accomplishments?

2. What motivates your "good deeds"?

3. What steps can you take to keep your motives on track—both as a coach and as a child of God?

### Workout

Acts 20:24; Galatians 2:19-20;
Philippians 3:7-11

### Overtime

*Please remind me, oh God, that nothing compares to knowing Christ Jesus my Lord! Amen.*

### Journal

**Journal**

**Note**

1. Oswald Chambers, *My Utmost for His Highest* (Grand Rapids, MI: Discovery House Publishers, 1992), n.p., emphasis added.

# 28

# How Big Is
# Your Jesus?

### Ready

*Before God and Christ Jesus, who is going to judge
the living and the dead, and by His appearing and
His kingdom, I solemnly charge you: proclaim the
message; persist in it whether convenient
or not; rebuke, correct, and encourage
with great patience and teaching.*

2 TIMOTHY 4:1-2

### Set

One day, I was leaving my office late after a
challenging afternoon. Just as I was locking the
door, a student whom I barely knew asked if I
were on my way home. My initial thought was
that since I'd already worked later than usual
and I was tired, I'd ask him to come back tomorrow. But I noticed something in his eyes, so
I unlocked my door and invited him in.

Then he stunned me with his question: He
wanted to know why I was always kind to him
and other athletes! Considering how only seconds earlier I was about to tell him to come back
later, I realized that I was being given an opportunity to tell a young man what motivated
me to care about him. As a result of staying

a few minutes late, I was able to share with him the good news of Jesus Christ, who cared so much for us that He took the punishment for our sins on Himself by going to the cross.

The opportunities that the Lord places in front of us might not always seem convenient, but they always have eternal significance. If we are to influence the people around us (particularly the athletes we coach), we must be ready—even when we'd rather do something else—to represent Christ by our words, thoughts and actions. We must yield to the person and work of Jesus living in us so that the people He sends our way are loved with His love. We never know how He might lead us! —*Ken Kladnik*

### Go

1. What are some opportunities that you have missed because of busyness?

2. Think about when you have made time for another person. What was the outcome?

3. How can your door be more open to others?

### Workout

Luke 10:38-42; Galatians 5:16-26;
Ephesians 5:1-2,15-16

### Overtime

*Lord, use me today to share the good news of Your kingdom. Help me to not allow the world's distractions to keep me from doing Your will. Thank You for each opportunity that will present itself as You lead me by Your Holy Spirit. Amen.*

### Journal

**Journal**

# 29

# Exit the
# Roller Coaster

### Ready

*About midnight Paul and Silas were praying
and singing hymns to God, and the [other]
prisoners were listening to them.*

ACTS 16:25

### Set

Whoever said life is a roller coaster must have
been a coach. It seems that on a daily basis, the
coaching profession can send us rocketing toward glorious, adrenaline-boosted highs. But it
can also throw us into a downward spiral with
exasperating emotional lows.

One of our best opportunities to be witnesses
to our players is to show them that, as Christians, our emotions aren't bound to these ups
and downs. If we appear to be exuberant when
we are winning but seem nearly suicidal after
a bad practice, we are not modeling the con-
sistent joy of Christ. Our players need to see
that our joy is not based on what they do or
do not do, but that it is based entirely on what
Christ did for us at Calvary. The reality of His
death and resurrection is the source of our daily
and eternal joy! That means we can honor God

on good and bad days. As author Jerry Bridges wrote, "The purpose of joy is to glorify God by demonstrating to an unbelieving world that our loving and faithful heavenly Father cares for us and provides for us all that we need."[1]

So let's exit the emotional roller coaster. Let's remember that Paul and Silas remained joyful throughout their imprisonment and sang praises to God in their jail cells because they knew in whom they had placed their faith! Surely, we too can remain joyful in Jesus throughout our seasons and give God the glory He deserves in our locker rooms! —*Chanda Husser Rigby*

### Go

1. Does your team feel like your happiness is based on its performance?

2. How can you exemplify that joy in Christ does not depend on any earthly circumstances?

3. Where does your joy come from?

### Workout

Psalms 43:1-5; 51:10-13; Philippians 4:11-13

### Overtime

*Eternal God, please fill me with Your everlasting joy so that my life might be a reflection of Your constant love. In Jesus' name, amen.*

**Journal**

**Journal**

**Note**
1. Jerry Bridges, *The Practice of Godliness* (Colorado Springs, CO: NavPress, 1996), p. 115.

# 30

# Wait on the Lord

### Ready

*But those who trust in the Lord will renew their strength; they will soar.*

ISAIAH 40:31

### Set

I took my first head-coaching job in 1982 at Hononegah High School in Rockton, Illinois. The girls' basketball program had been winless for three years. I walked into an environment that was in complete and utter disarray, and there were some very difficult young people involved in the program.

As we started that process, our team went through a step-by-step process and re-created the culture, the personality, and the character of our program. In our first year, we went 0-22. The following year, we won three games. The next year, we won 17 games. The next year, we won 21, we were conference champions and we advanced to the regional state basketball tournament. In four years, we made some very significant progress, but it was difficult and required an incredible amount of patience.

It's easy to get weary and discouraged when things don't happen immediately. We live in an instant society. We want it now. We want our hamburger in five minutes. We want our playing time now. We want our championship today. And because we're not patient, we get weaker and we begin to lose our resolve.

In Isaiah 40, the prophet reminds us that God will renew our strength when we are patient with Him and when we trust Him in everything. But trust is the key. We have to trust in our calling in order to have access to divine patience.

If trust is at the core of your relationship with God, then no matter how fast or slow, or how many days, weeks, months, years or decades it takes, you'll have to have the character and patience to wait on His eternal purposes.
—*Deb Patterson*

### Go

1. Have you been through a difficult circumstance that God used to teach you patience?

2. Read Isaiah 40:29-31. How does this Scripture give you encouragement to have patience and press on through difficult circumstances?

3. Is trust at the core of your relationship with God?

### Workout

Psalm 40; Proverbs 3:5-6; Isaiah 40:28-31

## Overtime

*Father, help me to be patient with Your plan
for my life. In the midst of difficult circumstances,
help me to trust in You and lean on You for strength
and guidance as You build me into the person
You want me to be. Amen.*

**Journal**

**Journal**

# 31

# Choosing Sides

### Ready

*You did not choose Me, but I chose you.
I appointed you that you should go out and
produce fruit, and that your fruit should
remain, so that whatever you ask the Father
in My name, He will give you.*

JOHN 15:16

### Set

When I was a kid, our neighborhood basketball court—the kind with the chain nets—was the place where everybody went to play the best basketball. During the summers, top college and high school players packed the court.

One day, I was chosen by a college player to be on his team—something I really didn't want to do. To me, the opposing team looked a lot more capable of winning. As I stood beside the college player, wishing that I were on the other team, he turned to me and said, "You don't want to be on our team, do you? I chose you, but I can tell that you don't want to be on our team." I hadn't said a word to him about it, but my body language had betrayed my thoughts. When he asked me if I wanted to be on the other team, I said yes. He responded, "Okay, go over there. We'll take Tommy instead." I went, and our team lost.

That college player, just by looking at me, could tell that I didn't want to commit to his team. When God chooses us and invites us to follow Him, thank goodness He doesn't change His mind if one day we don't look like we're much of a Christian! He never says, "Okay, go over there. I'll find someone else instead." In fact, the Bible says that He will leave the flock of 99 to search the hills for the one lost sheep (see Luke 15:4).

Even when we don't make winning decisions, Jesus Christ, our Good Shepherd, remains faithful in His devotion to us. His grace then becomes so irresistible that we'll never want to wander away from Him! And if for some reason we get a little distracted, He stands waiting for our return to His side. —*Les Steckel*

### Go

1. Do you base your daily decisions on Christ's commitment to you?

2. How can His devotion to you inspire devotion from you?

3. What does it feel like to be chosen by God?

### Workout

Joshua 24:14-15; John 15:11-17;
1 Corinthians 15:58

## Overtime

*Thank You, God, for seeking me and choosing me to be Your disciple! I ask that You would help me to bear fruit today that reflects Your devotion. Amen.*

### Journal

**Journal**

# Contributors

**Jane Albright** is the head women's basketball coach at the University of Nevada at Reno. In 25 years at the collegiate level, she has amassed over 400 career wins. While the head coach at Wisconsin, she led her team to the 2000 WNIT Championship and has taken her teams to a combined nine NCAA Tournament appearances. She is the all-time winningest coach at both Wisconsin and Northern Illinois.

**Cheryl Baird** was an All-American volleyball player at Wheaton College in Wheaton, Illinois, and has been an assistant coach with junior track and in college volleyball. She and her family reside in Wheaton.

**Dan Britton** serves as the Executive Vice President of International and Training at the FCA National Support Center in Kansas City, Missouri. In high school and college, Dan was a standout lacrosse player. Dan and his family reside in Overland Park, Kansas.

**Danny Burns** is the Director of Digital Ministry at FCA's National Support Center in Kansas City, Missouri. Danny helped lead the Northwest Missouri State Huddle as a varsity distance runner until 2004. A 2010 graduate of Calvary Theological Seminary, he's one of the pastors at Avenue Church. He, his wife, Ashley, and his family reside in the Kansas City area.

**Sherri Coale** is the head women's basketball coach at the University of Oklahoma where she has led the Sooners to four Big 12 tournament championships and six regular season titles. As of the end of the 2009-2010 season, Coale's teams have made the NCAA tournament 11 times, including three appearances in the Final Four. Coale is also a four-time Big 12 Coach of the Year.

**Tony Dungy** is the former head coach of the Indianapolis Colts. He led Indianapolis to victory at Super Bowl XLI and also played for the Pittsburgh Steelers team that won Super Bowl XIII. Dungy currently works as a studio football analyst for NBC.

**Clay Elliott** played pro baseball for five years in the Atlanta Braves organization. He joined the FCA staff in 1999 and is the FCA Director for Santa Clara County in Northern California.

**Joe Girardi** is the manager of the New York Yankees and a former 15-year veteran catcher. He has been a part of four World Series championship teams—three as a player (1996, 1998, 1999) and one as a manager (2009)—all as a member of the Yankees.

**Debbie Haliday** works as a staff associate in Women's Basketball at UCLA. She competed as a Bruin on both the women's championship-winning softball and basketball teams. Debbie also writes for wired4sport.com and leads teams into Baja, Mexico, doing camp ministry as "Jugamos." She is married to Lance Haliday and has three children: Matthew, Ryan and Bethany.

**Michael Hill** has served as a football coach at both the college and high school levels. He volunteers with FCA and lives with his family in Winfield, Kansas.

**Clint Hurdle** is the manager of the Pittsburgh Pirates. He previously managed the Colorado Rockies and led that franchise to its first National League pennant in 2007. As a player, Hurdle spent 10 years at the Major League level playing for Kansas City, Cincinnati, St. Louis and the New York Mets.

**Mike Jarvis** is the men's basketball coach at Florida Atlantic University. He previously coached at Boston University, George Washington University, and St. John's University, where he took his teams to a combined nine NCAA Tournaments. Jarvis led St. John's to the 2000 Big East regular season title, and in 1990 he was named America East Coach of the Year. Coach Jarvis is the only coach to win 100 games at three different universities and 100 games at the high school level.

**Susan Johnson** is the head women's basketball coach at Georgetown College in Georgetown, Kentucky. She has also served as the women's tennis coach and as a professor of kinesiology and health studies.

**Ken Kladnik** is a certified athletic trainer and the head athletic trainer at Central Washington University in Ellensburg, Washington. He is also active in FCA as a huddle coach.

**Roger Lipe** is the Southern Illinois representative for the FCA and serves as the chaplain for the Southern Illinois University athletic teams. He is also the author of several devotional books. Roger and his family live in Carbondale, Illinois.

**Kathy Malone** is a certified athletic trainer in a sports medicine clinic that serves several high schools in Indianapolis, Indiana. She is also an FCA volunteer and serves as chaplain for the WNBA's Indiana Fever.

**Donna Miller** is director of athletics at Mary Baldwin College in Staunton, Virginia. She previously coached intercollegiate tennis for 15 years with stints at Virginia Intermont College, Eastern Mennonite University and Mary Baldwin College.

**Tom Osborne** is the former head football coach at the University of Nebraska. Over 25 seasons, he led the Cornhuskers to three national championships (1994, 1995, 1997) and 13 combined Big 8 and Big 12 conference championships. Osborne also served a six-year term in the U.S. House of Representatives. He was most recently Nebraska's athletic director. He is the author of *Beyond the Final Score* and *Secrets to Becoming a Leader*.

**Deb Patterson** is the women's basketball coach at Kansas State University and a two-time Big 12 Coach of the Year. She has led the Wildcats to seven NCAA Tournament appearances through 2010 and a pair of Big 12 championships. Kansas State also won the 2006 WNIT title under her guidance.

**Lisa Phillips** serves as the varsity softball coach at Bremen High School in Bremen, Georgia. She is also the school's FCA huddle coach.

**Sue Ramsey** is the head women's basketball coach and senior women's administrator at Ashland University in Ohio. Coach Ramsey enjoys the opportunities to share with others as a motivational speaker.

**Chanda Husser Rigby** is the head women's basketball coach at Holmes Community College in Goodman, Mississippi, where she also serves as the FCA huddle coach.

**Al Schierbaum** coached baseball at Dallas Baptist University for 11 years and has coached two summer touring teams. He currently serves as the Great Lakes Regional Director for FCA. He and his family reside in Streetsboro, Ohio.

**Toby C. Schwartz** is the head cross country/track and field coach at Whitworth College in Spokane, Washington. In nine seasons, Toby has been recognized eight times as coach of the year. He has coached more than 65 national qualifiers and 12 All-Americans, including a national champion in the women's 100 meter in 2004.

**Sue Semrau** is the women's basketball coach at Florida State University, where she has won more games than any other coach in school history. Semrau was named the 2004, 2007 and 2009 ACC Coach of the Year and currently serves on the Board of Directors for the Women's Basketball Coaches Association.

**Mike Singletary** is a linebacker coach and an assistant to the head coach for the Minnesota Vikings, and also the former head coach of the San Francisco 49ers. A member of the Pro Football Hall of Fame, Singletary played 12 seasons with the Chicago Bears, where he was a member of the Super Bowl XX championship team. He is the co-author, with Jay Carty, of *Mike Singletary One-on-One*.

**Les Steckel** spent 30 years coaching football at the high school, college and professional levels (his teams at the professional level reached two Super Bowls). He currently serves as president/CEO of FCA. Les and his wife, Chris, reside in Overland Park, Kansas.

**Rex Stump** serves as the Area Director for the Buckeye Border (NW Ohio) FCA. A former high school coach and pastor for 20 years, Rex serves in the ministries of FCA, pastors a church, coaches youth sports, and chaplains multiple teams. He is blessed to be married to his great wife, Jenny, and they have three active boys: Collin, Carter and Clay.

# Thanks

### Thanks from FCA to:

Donna Noonan, Bethany Hermes,
Teri Wolfgang, Ashley Grosse, Jill Ewert
and everyone who worked tirelessly
to make this project happen.

To all the athletes and coaches who are:
Sharing Christ boldly;
Seeking Christ passionately;
Leading others faithfully;
and Loving others unconditionally.

To Bill Greig III, Stan Jantz, Kim Bangs,
Rob Williams and Carol Eide at Regal Books.

To all FCA staff across the country who
demonstrate integrity, serving, teamwork
and excellence as they work to see the
world impacted for Jesus Christ.

# Impacting the World for Christ Through Sports

**FELLOWSHIP OF
CHRISTIAN ATHLETES**

Since 1954, the Fellowship of Christian Athletes has challenged athletes and coaches to impact the world for Jesus Christ. FCA is cultivating Christian principles in local communities nationwide by encouraging, equipping, and empowering others to serve as examples and make a difference. FCA reaches approximately 2 million people annually on the professional, college, high school, junior high and youth levels. Through FCA's Four Cs of Ministry—coaches, campus, camps, and community—and the shared passion for athletics and faith, lives are changed for current and future generations.

### FCA's Four Cs of Ministry

**Coaches:** Coaches are the heart of FCA. Our role is to minister to them by encouraging and equipping them to know and serve Christ. FCA ministeres to coaches through Bible studies, prayer support, discipleship and mentoring, resources, outreach events and retreats. FCA values coaches, first for who they are, and for what God has created them to do.

**Campus:** The Campus Ministry is initiated and led by student-athletes and coaches on junior high, high school and college campuses. The Campus Ministry types—Huddles, Team Bible Studies, Chaplain Programs and Coaches Bible Studies—are effective ways to establish FCA ministry presence, as well as outreach events such as One Way 2 Play-Drug Free programs, school assemblies and Fields of Faith.

**Camp:** Camp is a time of "inspiration and perspiration" for coaches and athletes to reach their potential by offering comprehensive athletic, spiritual and leadership training. FCA offers seven types of camps: Sports Camps, Leadership Camps, Coaches Camps, Power Camps, Partnership Camps, Team Camps and International Camps.

**Community:** With the majority of athletes playing sports in the community (non-campus programs), FCA is ministering to the club, recreational and youth sports teams with the goal of establishing on-going ministry for coaches and athletes to compete for Jesus Christ with character, passion and excellence.